The Adventures of Indigo

By Kathryn Phillips

Illustrated by Julia Reynolds

Library of Congress

Copyright 2006

Phillips, Kathryn

The Adventures of Indigo

Total Behavior Management
A division of Phillips Associates, LLC

ISBN 0-9776218-3-9

The Adventures of Indigo

By Kathryn Phillips

Illustrated by Julia Reynolds

Technical assistance by Steve Talbott

For people and balloons all over the world in search of self

Once upon a time in a city not too far away, on the city's busiest street corner, there worked a peddler. From his brightly colored cart came the most ordinary kitchen utensils, hairbrushes, cat collars, poodle pajamas, and stale pretzels. As you might well guess, these items were not particularly interesting to the shoppers, especially with all the modern stores around. Had it not been for the assortment of brightly colored balloons that flew from one pillar of his cart, the peddler would have had no business at all. You see, the balloons attracted the children of the city, who in turn brought their mothers, who in turn felt obliged to buy something from the old peddler. It was a good business as far as the peddler was concerned, but there were other opinions to consider.

Ever since Indigo could remember, it had not been easy being a balloon. There are so many small things that neither you nor I could ever understand, having never been balloons ourselves. Hardly a day went by when the peddler didn't yank on Indigo's knot so hard that he thought he would burst. Common was the child who would beg his mother for a balloon, only to stomp on it immediately just to hear the popping sound it made. One of Indigo's cousins, in fact, got his start (and sadly his end) at a birthday party during which the children blew him and others up, tied them to their ankles, and had a race to see how fast they could pop one another's balloons. In the end there was nothing but a mass of shredded rubber and broken string, while the children ran off to feed themselves full of ice cream and cake (as if one would have an appetite after such an ordeal). Indigo shuddered at the very thought. At times, Indigo considered himself lucky to be the dark blue color he was. Most children preferred the sky blue color of Frank or Marissa, or the cherry red of Rosada, or the lime green of LaWanda. Most of the time, Indigo knew that his less desirable coloring was much to his advantage, especially when a particularly mean child came to purchase a balloon. But not being wanted by a child was almost as discouraging as being sold. Because of his unusual coloring and somewhat lopsided shape (when the peddler blew him up he failed to fill Indigo entirely, leaving a small, pointed pocket that had not been blown into shape), Indigo was not often invited to join in many balloon-type activities. While the other balloons chatted and played games, Indigo spent his days apart, humming melodies that he made up, and thinking of far away lands. He sang and dreamt and wished and hummed, for Indigo knew that what he really wanted was to be free of the strings that tied him to the peddler's cart and the worries of troublesome existence.

One day, such as the one I have described to you here, a particularly mean looking child came up to the peddler's cart. There was a murmur among the balloons as they whispered their fears at the possibility of being sold to this sour-looking youngster. He looked, you see, very much like the type who delighted in birthday parties and LOUD, popping noises. The thought sent a shiver through Indigo, leaving him feeling cold and lonesome. Perhaps his uncommon color would save him again, as it had many times in the past. It was not long before a hush settled over the balloons, as each one waited in the uneasy silence to see whose string would be tugged, setting the bright shape to bounce helplessly in the still blue sky.

It was hardly a tug that Indigo felt at that moment. It was a jerk. A mean, purposeful, deliberate jerk. He felt his face flush with anger and helplessness as he bobbed uncontrollably in the wind. The excited murmuring began once more among the balloons:

"At least it was only Indigo."

"Yes, good riddance I say!"

"Always a loner anyway."

The murmurings grew fainter as the boy danced along the crowded sidewalk and rounded the corner. At last, mercifully, the sight of the peddler's stand faded away and the boy and Indigo were alone. A deafening silence filled the air and made Indigo shudder down to his very string. His mother had warned him there would come a day like this; however, there was hardly time to reminisce about his mother. Indigo's thoughts were continually interrupted by harsh tugs on his string, pulling him closer and closer to the rough cement of the sidewalk, getting him into position for the delightful popping sound for which the boy had saved his allowance all week to hear. The scratchy sidewalk began to stretch and pull at his delicate rubber shell. It was to be a cruel and tragic ending. He tried desperately to think of something happy, a song perhaps, but only glimpses of his life flashed across his mind. He thought of the first day the peddler blew him up, and the time he was given his very own string. He thought of the day when his father and mother were sold to a gentle elderly couple that, he knew, would take good care of them. Those had been happy times—times of faith and hope for the future. But now there was no future, no faith, and certainly no hope.

It was just as these thoughts were running through Indigo's mind that a most unusual thing happened. It was not that breezes were uncommon to this city, but certainly this particular afternoon had been almost deathly still, so the slightest breeze seemed oddly out of place. Yet, a soft, gentle breeze softened the air, so lightly that it was barely noticeable at first. For a moment it seemed that time had stood still. Quickly, though, this breeze began to grow and grow. It began to pick up its pace, and soon the breeze turned from a sleeping lamb to a roaring tiger! Huge gusts ravaged the trees. The peddler's common kitchen utensils toppled over one another. Old men grabbed their hats and ladies grabbed their skirts. Children ran clinging to their mothers. Cats and dogs scurried under the peddler's cart and, for a brief time, shared shelter with one another.

It is not hard to guess what happened next. The merciless child, who had gripped Indigo with such force, instinctively reached for his cap, releasing Indigo in the process! In an instant, the deep blue, misshaped sphere was

carried up, up, up into the freedom of the light blue sky.

5

It was a few minutes before Indigo realized what was happening, as the gusts of wind carried him far above the city's noise and confusion.

"This is exciting indeed! Rather awkward, of course…," Indigo nervously chuckled to himself, "not at all unpleasant, but certainly awkward." He rolled on his back, and then on his front, and then on his back again, beaming into the brilliant sunshine.

"Ah yes, that's it!" he muttered as he positioned himself. Far below, he saw Frank and Marissa and Rosada and even Lawanda straining their strings to see Indigo sail like a delicate blue cloud in a sea of white pillows. He could even see the boy who had bought him, jumping up and down in a fury, demanding that his money be returned. It was a glorious view. Exhilaration filled his heart and soul as he soared unattached from the peddler's cart. In fact, he felt so free and joyous that a song just popped into his head. It went something like this:

Biddle dee bop
Biddle dee bop
Greetings to you
The sun and the wind too
Biddle dee bop Biddle de bop
Take me so far
To touch the stars and planets

And Mars
And moons and goons
And Septembers and Junes
And to think it's just me
a silly balloon!

Just then, a hushed, almost breathless voice seemed to come from nowhere and everywhere all at once. "You are very welcome, Indigo," said the Voice.

"What was that?" Indigo bolted upright briefly, losing his airborne balance. "I thought I heard a voice," he paused, listening intently. But, after a moment of silence, he said to himself, "Nope. I must just be hearing things," and settled back, somewhat puzzled.

"Indigo…" It came again.

"What? Someone is definitely talking to me! I hear it again!" He strained again to listen for what was not really a voice, but more like a whisper, more like air, yes, more like words in air.

"Who is there?" Indigo demanded.

"Indigo…"

"Yes?" Indigo replied in a hesitant and shaky voice.

"Indigo. It is I, the Wind," said the Voice in a tone so deep and gentle it verged on being spiritual.

"The what?" asked Indigo. "The wind? Now that is an interesting thought! Actually it is the most ridiculous thing I've heard, but nonetheless interesting. How could it be that air would speak? I shall someday have to make up a song about that. Let's see…" the balloon chuckled, finally feeling a little less shaken.

"Indigo," the Voice persisted, "many times I have spoken to you. I am the air that rushes past on chilly winter days. I am the gentle breeze that cools you on sultry summer nights. I am that which rustles the trees and stirs the leaves. I am …The Wind."

There was a long silence—a pause so deep that it could have filled an ocean. It was Indigo who was the first to speak.

"Then I do thank you, Wind," said he, "for saving my life. You are very kind. But if you will pardon me, I must be on my way. I have far away lands to discover and important things to do."

"And I do not?" asked the Wind flatly. Again a silence weighed heavy in the air. This time it was the breathless Voice that broke the spell. "My dear Indigo," the Voice sighed, "you have so much to learn. The life of a wanderer is much more complex than you may choose to believe. I have come," he paused, "to be your teacher. To free you from the string that ties you to the peddler's cart. I have come to teach your soul to dance and your bright blue shape to fly. Come, Indigo, be a student of the Wind."

Indigo glanced around him. If this was some kind of joke, it certainly wasn't very funny. Air that speaks? Free me from my strings? My soul? What, pray tell, is a Soul? I don't even think I have a soul, thought he.

"And what if I choose not to follow you, Mr. Wind? What then?" he asked in a hesitant voice that sounded strangely unfamiliar to him.

"Then you shall be left to accept the fate of your own decision." It was not a threat that the Wind spoke to Indigo; rather, it sounded like a statement from one who had lived the past and could see the future. One so great and wise it was difficult to believe that he was speaking to this bumbling naïve balloon. It was then that Indigo decided that to be in good favor with the Wind could not be a poor idea.

And that, my friend, is how Indigo and the Wind came into acquaintance. As the Wind carried Indigo along on a gentle, warm breeze, bouncing his blue shape through the clouds, Indigo gazed at what lay below him. He admired lazy, rolling hills and patchwork farmlands, many colorful communities and contrasting deep blue rivers snaking their way through the lands. The sight was one to fill Indigo with wonder and awe, and at times it rendered him speechless (which you can believe is most unusual for Indigo). He hummed his songs and rocked to the gentle rhythm of the breeze as the Wind weaved him throughout the clouds. From time to time, Indigo would find some playful cloud to engage in a game of hide-and-go-seek. The clouds nearly always won, much to Indigo's consternation (balloons are well know for being sore losers). The Wind told Indigo stories of people and places and wonderful activities for which the Wind provided power, like kite flying and sailing adventures, and even great races! Indigo could hardly contain himself when he thought of all that he had yet to experience.

Sometimes the Wind would all but stop for a moment or two. The Wind, being millions of years old, tired rarely, but was not invincible. At these times Indigo would find himself falling fast to earth. Fear would grip his heart and he would cry out for help, only to discover that the Wind had rejuvenated his strength and begun to lift him to a new height. Indigo was learning to depend on the mighty Wind, and the Wind accepted his responsibility, as well.

It was a joyful time, for it was not long before the Wind and Indigo became friends, as well as expert travel companions. At times the Wind wondered what had come over him that peaceful afternoon to invest in a travel companion as awkward and bumbling as Indigo. But Indigo brought a sparkle and innocence to the wise old Wind— something that had been missing from his life for a few thousand years.

Those first few weeks of travel, Indigo learned a lot about the world. In his young, sheltered life with the peddler, the balloon only dreamed of what existed beyond the busy street corner. Now he found himself drifting powerlessly above a much larger world than he had ever imagined.

The Wind, Indigo discovered, was even wiser than he had guessed him to be that first day they met. Oftentimes he would seem to read Indigo's thoughts and answer unspoken questions about the lands he gazed upon far below. The mighty mountains and the curving rivers each had a wonderful story which the Wind was eager to tell. He related stories of when, in the beginning, the earth was a mass of gasses and fire. He explained that over time, with his help, this fire had cooled, leaving the earth in the shapes that Indigo saw below. He told of the first birds, loud squawking creatures with great wingspans. They were not nearly as graceful as those you see today, but being the first of their kind, the Wind had thought them beautiful and had gazed upon them with admiration.

One of the Wind's greatest tales was about the Great Ice Age. Long ago the entire planet began to freeze, he told Indigo, leaving everything from the tiniest one-celled animal to the greatest of dinosaurs to die in the frozen wasteland. It was clear to Indigo that it had been a sad time in the Wind's existence. The Wind felt a deep loneliness for the creatures that had once inhabited the earth and filled the skies (not unlike balloons or people, the Wind needed companionship).

In the echo of the Wind's story, Indigo remembered how the peddler used to sell flavored ice on stifling summer days. The icy treat had been almost as well liked as the balloons, and was a friend to the children. It was difficult to imagine ice and snow being the enemy, a purveyor of tragedy, and a killer of one's friends. The Wind paused briefly to contemplate his explanation, and then said:

"Indigo, I shall take you to a place that resembles those days of ice and cold. It is a frozen wasteland in which few humans have learned to live." His tone was sad as he continued, "My bitter cold winds cloud their days and fill their nights. It is a prison, surrounded by nothing but ice and cold, a great distance from here."

In the silence, one could almost hear the Wind lament over the painful memories. Without another word the pair set out on their journey to the barren land.

True to his word, the Wind and Indigo traveled quite a distance to their destination. The Wind was a gentle, yet chilling breeze that carried the balloon steadily. The journey left the Wind strangely silent and serious. In spite of better judgment, Indigo grew bored and impatient.

"Are we there yet, Wind? When will we be there? How much longer do we have to go? Shall I sing a song to make the time pass? I know a lovely 'Snow Song'." There was hardly even a sigh from the great teacher, but Indigo could feel the air around him turn progressively cooler as they neared the icy land. Indigo had learned early that complaining was something that Wind simply would not tolerate, so he made no mention of the fact that he felt the air inside him beginning to freeze. He felt his string turn icy as they hovered over the flat, barren land covered with the white crunchy stuff the peddler had once sold. There were drab shacks dotting the plains, a testimony to the fact that people did indeed live there. The sight chilled him and the Snow Song was soon forgotten.

At last his thoughts were interrupted by a chuckle from the Wind. "Look over there, friend. A child, skating on the ice!" As soon as he spoke, Indigo saw a child, bundled so thickly that she looked like a miniature polar bear balancing on the steel blades of her skates. She moved about the ice slowly, but gracefully for one who resembled a polar bear. She swayed to and fro, cutting delicate shapes in the frozen surface. When she saw Indigo, she began at once to wave. A warmth crept over him as he smiled and waved his icy string back at her. What a loving child, he thought. She was not at all like the ones he had known when he was under the peddler's care. Children, then, had been something to fear, but this one seemed warm and gentle and kind. "I must have a closer look at this child," he thought, "I must…"

As if reading his thoughts, the Wind answered: "Do not go any closer. It might be dangerous…"

"Wind, you are wrong," he interrupted. "This child is not dangerous; she is loving. Please take me close. You'll see." There were times (and this was certainly one of them) when Indigo's persistence could not be avoided.

"So be it," the Wind said crisply. Without another word, a whoosh came down from behind Indigo and a whirling breeze sent him spinning. It whooshed and whirled him around until he was dizzy and wobbling through the cold air toward the child. In an instant Indigo was within the child's reach, and she called to him. At this distance, what he saw was a beautiful child with pink skin and twinkling blue eyes, a child filled with laughter and warmth. It was a happy feeling just to be near this little girl, to be so close that Indigo was surrounded by her innocence and light.

Unfortunately, Indigo had overlooked the razor sharp icicles that hung from the tree near the child. Having a threatening look to them, like monster's fangs, they glistened in the light. Still unaware, he drifted nearer and nearer to the child, full of anticipation. The child saw them, though, and let out a helpless cry. She pointed frantically at the icicles, and began jumping up and down in excitement and fear. Indigo, thinking that she was just terribly excited to see him, moved faster, eagerly smiling from side to side.

"Look OUT!!!" the girl screamed in one final attempt to stop him. Only then did he swivel himself to see the swords of ice moving in for the kill. Panic overcame him. His eyes widened into saucers and his mouth opened down to his knot. The formerly enticing presence of the child was forgotten in the rush of his words:

"Wind! SAVE MEEEE!" His string was nearly touching them now! No thin rubber balloon could fight these icy spears; it was sure to mean …. he couldn't stand it any longer. In desperation he squeezed his eyes tightly, as if to shut out impending fate. And then, a tremendous "WOOSH!" resounded over the ice.

It was the same gust of wind that had saved Indigo's life on that busy sidewalk—a gust so great it seemed to rattle the earth and the air. It whooshed and swirled and sent the little girl flying. It blew the snow and shook the icicles until they knocked against one another in a rattling percussion.

It lifted Indigo up and far away from the snow and the little girl with the dancing eyes. Below, Indigo saw the icicles that had made the deafening sound as they crashed to the ice, barely missing him as he tossed and turned in the wind. His entire sphere trembled.

It was a long while before the Wind spoke again. The curious balloon pondered the embarrassing lesson he had just learned. The mighty Wind was not only wise, but compassionate, as well. He had saved Indigo from death now for the second time, even though it meant chilling the frozen land with his mighty gusts. It had been an act of kindness and love that the little balloon would not soon forget.

With time, and much silence, Indigo and his teacher drifted from the cold wasteland toward cities and villages. Indigo's string began to thaw, and it wasn't long before he was ready for more stories and adventures from the Great Wind. Below him he saw green meadows filled with wild flowers and mountains, whose jagged peaks were frosted with snow. In the villages, the houses were very different from the grey cement ones Indigo had seen from the peddler's cart.

These houses were painted with colorful designs decorating their shudders and window boxes. The streets were made of old crumbling bricks. As the people walked, it made a cheerful clop! clop! clop! sound beneath their wooden shoes. The Wind blew him toward the canals that meandered through the center of the city. On them were the boats whose bottoms were made of glass. Windmills dotted the countryside and bright red and yellow flowers grew abundantly. Here the Wind was a welcome friend. He made the wheels of the windmills turn, giving power to the people of the villages.

He made the children's kites fly, and the birds soar, and the leaves dance. He was, after all, The Wind.

There were times when Indigo forgot that he was really only a balloon, really just a thin rubber shell filled with nothing but air, with a lifeless string holding him together, keeping all that he had inside of him. He had become a part of the Wind, the air, and the universe. He drifted along under the gentle power of his companion and became a piece of the sky. Yes, it was easy to forget.

One day, however, a lazy drifting sort of day, a brilliant orange shape appeared over the horizon. As it neared, Indigo could faintly read some writing printed across the top of the bubble. It appeared to be a balloon with an inscription. In bright bold letters was the word "Ziggy" printed across the forlorn balloon.

How nice, thought Indigo, to have your name printed right there on your shape! What a delightful idea. A very fashionable one, indeed. Perhaps I'll surprise the Wind by having *my name* inscribed on *myself* (it should be noted that balloons could be very vain at times).

As the balloon neared, Indigo called out to him,

"Top of the day to you, Mr. Ziggy! I trust your name is Ziggy?"

"No," sniffed the balloon, seemingly offended. "That is not my name." He turned around to show his backside. Across the orange rubber in even bolder letters was printed: "ZIGGY'S SUPERMARKET GRAND OPENING."

"It is not easy being a promotional balloon, you know," he sighed as he passed Indigo. "One never really finds one's own identity."

18

Long after the bright orange balloon disappeared over the horizon, Indigo questioned the wise old Wind on the meaning of the balloon's words.

"What did he mean, Wind, by having an identity? Is it a fatal illness one contracts? Or a feature one possesses? Or a growth? Do I have an identity? Or two or maybe three?"

"No," chuckled the Wind ,"it is not a disease, nor is it a growth like having a nose or two eyes." And then in a serious tone he said, "It is not a matter of simply finding an identity. Rather it is a feeling that grows over time and with a deep knowing of who one is and who one is intended to be. It is a loyalty and truth to oneself."

It was the kind of commentary that the Wind delivered upon occasion. It made little sense to Indigo at the moment, but he held it inside and hoped someday he would fully understand the meaning of the Wind's words.

20

Days passed and the evening skies were filled with vivid pinks and purples as they drifted towards the setting sun each evening. When there were no clouds for the Wind to blow away, he and his friend drifted aimlessly, gawking at the beauty of the evening. Sometimes in the twilight, Indigo would teach the Wind the songs that he had composed. The Wind joined joyfully, chuckling and making up words of his own. They were lightly dancing melodies that whispered through the trees and gently nudged the clouds to drift. Indigo even made up a song just for his friend and sang it to the clouds and stars. It went something like this:

If only you knew	And then we three	And if there were more
(Biddle dee bee)	(Biddle dee bee)	(Biddle dee bee)
My friend so true	Would sail the seas,	We'd settle on four.
(Biddle dee bee)	(Biddle dee bee)	(Biddle dee bee)
Surely then you	And go as we please	We'd see countries galore
(Biddle dee bee)	(Biddle dee bee)	(Biddle dee bee)
Would like him too.	You two and me	We three and one more.

Depending on how long Indigo's voice lasted, with the Wind sometimes singing in harmony, this particular song had up to ninety-four verses. "Not bad for a silly little balloon," thought Indigo, "not bad at all."

The duo drifted and dozed and sang until the sun shone on them and warmed Indigo's thin rubber shell. The days passed and the time became unimportant. Everything became a blur of sunshine and happiness and warmth.

This was not to say, however, that their lives were uneventful. One day it rained—a soft, steady rain that caused all the birds to take flight in search of shelter. When they saw Indigo, though, their curiosity was immediately aroused. What could this fat, blue bubble be doing way up in the sky? In wonderment, they began dodging and darting at Indigo, attempting to peck here and there at his pudgy tummy. It was a frightening situation indeed, as Indigo realized that just one well-placed peck could mean the end for him. After what seemed like a very long time of dodging and darting, the rain stopped, and the sun shown brightly. A rainbow formed and Indigo was able to hide himself in the splendid blue of the colorful rays. At last the menacing birds became confused and left. Then Indigo gratefully thanked the rainbow with a song as it faded away into the evening sky.

"Do you really think they will be there, Wind? Mercy, I am so excited I think I may burst if we don't get there soon!" Indigo trembled with excitement as he scurried behind the Wind. It was Thursday, the second of the month to be exact. It was the day of the Great Race. Indigo had been looking forward to this day since the Wind had first mentioned it a long time ago. Now that the day had finally arrived, he was certain that something was going to go wrong.

"The Wind is rarely mistaken," said his friend, rather offended at Indigo's pessimism.

"What are they like, Wind? What do they look like? Will they chat with me? Do they hum songs like we do?" Too many questions from Indigo made the Wind less apt to give answers. After interminable silence it became frustratingly clear that Indigo would have to wait and see for himself (provided that he did not burst with excitement beforehand).

Sailing over the horizon, Indigo weaved in and out of the clouds, humming songs to himself. Going somewhere with the Wind often took days, but Indigo loved long journeys. To him, getting there was half of the excitement. There was always a new song to be sung, a stray kite to play with, and always a cloud to hide behind.

"Ah, yes," said the Wind after an eternity of silent anticipation, "I believe I see them now." Gradually, over the horizon, the skies in the distance revealed a medley of bobbing, brilliant colors. The Great Balloon Race was about to begin. Starting from one ocean and racing to the other, the race was expected to take days. It promised to be a long and exhausting race, but without the Wind the race could not begin at all. Indigo knew that he was in the presence of a much honored guest.

The air near the starting point was filled with festivity and excitement. Rows of bright colors lined the clouds. Children's voices cheered gleefully. It was a sight to behold. Indigo knew then that it had been worth the wait.

"Ladies and Gentlemen," boomed the voice over the loudspeaker, "the honorable and distinguished Wind has arrived! We may begin the race!" With great ceremony, the Wind encircled the balloons along the jagged coastline and, clearing his throat, gave a majestic *whoosh*.

AND THEY WERE OFF!

The sky looked like a kaleidoscope as the colorful masses filled the sky and began moving in every direction at once. They weaved their way through the clouds with Indigo hot on their trail. Laughter and joy filled his heart as he danced through the sky among his strong, experienced brothers. It was very hard for him to be patient, but there were humans who hung below in small baskets that seemed even more impatient than Indigo. Occasionally he would catch bits of their conversations.

"Hey, Harry! Let out some air…. Yup, yup, little more…. All right, ease it down. Too Much!!!! Blimey, can't these blasted things go any faster?"

In a way Indigo felt sorry for the balloons, for they were certainly hurrying as fast as they could. But Indigo realized that only another balloon could understand. In his drifting, Indigo also caught bits of conversation between the balloons themselves.

"I wish he would quit yanking on my left rear rope. I AM hurrying! Would ya take it easy, fella?"

However, in the midst of the entire hubbub, it was a much smaller voice that caught Indigo's attention.

It came from a little (and rather tattered) balloon that was already lagging behind the others. But perhaps that is because the balloon was busy singing a resounding chorus of Biddle Dee Bops!!

"Good afternoon!" Indigo said brightly as he neared the humming balloon. "Indigo is my name!"

The ballon stopped shortly and blinked her eyes shyly. "Hullo, my name is Madeline. I hope I didn't disturb you with my humming."

"Not at all," said Indigo. "On the contrary, I thought I might be so bold as to join you in your chorus of Biddle Dee Bops. Have you ever tried Shoo Pop Shoo Pops? They give a delightful jazz sound to the melody. But first, I must ask you, what is the cause of the sadness that clouds your lovely eyes?" An embarrassed blush crept over the large balloon's shape, starting at the base of her rope and spreading upward to the very peak of her shape.

"I have been adrift for many years," she said sadly. "We have seen a great many races such as these, but my master is getting too old to fly me anymore. And I," the balloon glanced down at her tattered cloths, "have seen better days. This shall be our last race together. He has been very kind to me." She glanced down at the man occupying the basket below her. As if to convince Indigo that she was not saddened by this prospect, she feigned resolve and said brightly, "There is no use being sad. Shall we finish the Bee Bops?"

"Yes, certainly," agreed Indigo, trying to remain cheerful himself. And with that, the new friends sang loudly and joyously in silent agreement that it was best to mask the worries of the larger balloon.

Indigo noticed that Madeline's master was a spry old man with silver grey hair and twinkling brown eyes that seemed to dance at the very thought of the adventure he was undertaking. He himself hummed a tune, though not quite as imaginative as Biddle Dee Bop. He seemed unconcerned that he was drifting farther and farther away from his competitors. Madeline was right; he seemed to be a most kind and gentle man, but the words of his new friend echoed in his mind. This was to be the old man's last race. Indigo began to think that it was a shame to watch such a determined duo lose in such an obvious way.

As Indigo drifted upward in contemplation, a soft breeze whispered to him, "Indigo, my friend, you need to help them." He tried to shrug off this suggestion, but suddenly an idea came to him. Many times the Wind had watched tugboats along the river pull larger ships filled with cargo. The Wind had explained to Indigo that it was easy for the small tug to glide through the water. Once this motion was combined with the movement of a larger ship, the two could depend on each other's momentum to sail down the river. If this could work in water, thought Indigo, why not in the air? The idea appealed to Indigo as he flew up to tell Madeline about his plan.

"I don't know, Indigo," Madeline said after contemplating the plan for a few minutes. "I do want to play fairly...but on the other hand...," tears glistened in her lovely eyes, "to see my master finish his last race with pride and dignity would give me great joy."

And so, secretly, the two began to prepare Indigo's plan for action. Indigo floated down to where the old man's back was turned, and carefully wrapped his string around one of the huge ropes. With a great deal of effort (and perhaps a bit of help from the watching Wind) Indigo felt a budge. Slowly and carefully, the threesome began to move through the sky. It was not long before they cut through the clouds with a surprising amount of speed. Madeline began humming a song, and Indigo joined gleefully as he glanced up from his perch occasionally to see his friend beam brilliantly in the sunshine. Even Madeline's master began jumping up and down in excitement.

"Golly jeepers!" the old man cried, "I haven't gone this fast since the race back in '41! Go, Madeline, Go!!!!"

The enthusiasm was contagious. Indigo raced and Madeline strained her ropes with her very best effort. In rapid time the other contestants began to reappear on the horizon. They were catching up! It wouldn't be long at all until they were right up with the rest of the group!

But at that very moment, something dreadfully unexpected happened. With all of the excitement and pulling on Indigo's string, no one had noticed that his string had begun to rub against Madeline's rope, cutting itself on the rough surface. In one terrible, unforgettable moment, the little string was sliced through, right next to the rubber knot. The air inside him began to flush out! It sent the poor balloon into a tailspin, tossing it uncontrollably back and forth in the atmosphere. He shouted helplessly into the Wind for someone to save him, but it was too late.

The world began to fade into a hazy grey color.

When Indigo, awoke, he saw the old man bending over him and looking concerned. The kindly man struggled to fill Indigo with his air, and gently retied his knot, and then tore off a piece of his shirt to use as a new string for Indigo. The old man's hands were warm and gentle on Indigo's aching body. He was thankful for the man's care. As he glanced around, he saw Madeline resting nearby in a grassy field. She looked relieved when she saw Indigo open his eyes and blink in the bright sunshine. A soft Wind swirled the dust around him and tugged gently at his new string. All around him the Wind whispered, "You'll be fine, Indigo. You just took a nasty fall."

"But you and Madeline…," Indigo looked weakly at the old man, "you lost the race. You gave up the race to save me?"

The old man's eyes twinkled. "My little friend, Madeline has told me of your noble deed. We have not lost. We have won, because we have found a friend. Thank you, little one. Thank you so much."

With that, the Wind gently found Indigo and lifted him from the old man's hands. Indigo soared to new heights at the will of the Wind. "Goodbye!" he waved as a tear fell from his eye. "Goodbye Madeline, I will never forget you! "

For a long time, Indigo slept. He had been through an experience he would not soon forget, and he was exhausted. But after some time, Indigo awoke and found himself changed in very small ways. It was not that he had fresh air inside of him, nor that his once thin string had been replaced by a strip from the old man's tattered shirt, but he had changed in ways that one cannot always see.

"Wind," said Indigo rather sadly, "I will miss Madeline and her master. I feel rather empty inside, as thought there really is nothing in me but air. Sometimes I feel as if I have everything inside of me that a human being does, a heart for feeling…," he mused, "but today I feel empty."

"Ah, little balloon," said the Wind kindly, "it is a thing called loneliness that you feel. It is a longing deep down inside."

"Yes!" said Indigo, "That is the very word – longing. Does one only feel this for friends with whom he can no longer be?"

"No," began the Wind slowly, "it can be a longing for that which was and may never be again. One can also feel loneliness for time and circumstance."

"I don't understand, Wind. Time and circumstance? How can one feel lonely and sad for time?"

"Not time presently, Indigo, time that once was. Let me tell you a story, my friend. Maybe then you will understand."

Indigo settled back on a cloud to listen. The Wind's stories always promised to be soothing. He told them so beautifully.

"A long, long time ago…"

"Before I was born?"

"Yes, before you were born…there was a peaceful village. Near this village, on the very edge of town, there stood a forest. This forest was so deep and stood so tall that the people of the village often feared it. Every afternoon at about half past two, like clockwork, a strange and haunting melody came from the forest. Although beautiful, the melody frightened the people of the village tremendously, and no one dared to go near the source of the music. Many legends were told as to the source of the haunting melody, but there was little truth to them. Years went by, and the people of the village continued to avoid the forest. They only ventured near enough to gather some wood to burn, and logs to build their houses. And every day the beautiful music filled the air. Over the years, the little village grew and grew. More people with more children moved in and settled near the deep forest. More trees were needed to build things to keep the village growing into a prosperous city. A slow and gradual change began to happen during this time. Where once the haunting, beautiful music had been strong and melodic, it now grew weaker and less beautiful. Had whatever inhabited the forest grown old and weak? Too old and weak to exude the lovely music any longer?

"One day the leader of the village called for all the strong men that lived near the forest.

'You must go and find the strange creature that is in the forest and bring it back to me. We must know what makes this music.' With that, the men set out to find the source of the song. Many of them feared what they might find. It was weeks before the group arrived back with the much-awaited news. The mysterious melody was both elusive and dangerous. Things did not look hopeful.

'What do you mean?' cried the leader of the village, 'You cannot find it? That is nonsense! What other news have you to report?' he demanded.

'Sir,' the bravest of the men stepped forward, 'we have found that the forest is much smaller than ever before. The strange monster that sings the melody is making the forest disappear! Soon it will take over our village as well!'

There was a great commotion between the leader and his men. 'What!' he raged 'How can this be?' We must get rid of the monster so that our village is once again safe for our women and children!' With that, the leader ordered the men to cut down the entire forest to rid the village of this destructive monster.

"Without hesitation, great armies of men moved into the forest and proceeded to cut it down. They left behind nothing but jagged stumps and broken limbs in place of the once majestic forest. With the last falling tree, the haunting melody ceased indeed.

"Arriving back in the village, the brave men spoke to the leader once more: 'We have done what you ordered, Sir. We have cut down the entire forest, and the music has stopped. But,' he said tentatively, 'we still found no monster.' There was a murmuring within the crowd, then silence. They all watched as a little boy boldly stepped forward.

"'Good Sir,' he said, 'forgive my youth and innocence, but what is it that you have gained through this destruction? You have cut down your lovely forest, and the beautiful music has stopped. But you found no monster. Could it be that we ourselves are our own monster?' The murmuring began once more.

"'Silence,' said the leader, 'let the boy speak! Go on son...'

"'Many nights, I lie in my bed and strain to hear the music that the Wind sings through the trees outside my window. It is a sound that is both strangely beautiful and haunting. Could it be the Wind we fear?'

"There was suddenly great silence and sadness among the village people, for there was truth and wisdom in the little boy's words."

Indigo was still pondering the message of the story when the Wind interrupted his thoughts, "So you see Indigo, loneliness can be a longing for many things. Unfortunately, the human beings have not learned this lesson well. They cut down the forest and long for the song it sung. They dirty the waters and still wish to retrieve the fish that have died. They scar the land, and move mountains in the name of progress, and then weep at the ugliness they have caused. It brings me great sadness," sighed the Wind. "Look below and you will see."

Below him Indigo saw smokestacks blowing great clouds of billowing smoke, piles of rusting metal from aged, orphaned cars, and the great bulldozers scarring the land to make room for new houses and buildings.

"What has happened, Wind? Why do humans do this?"

There was no reply. The answer would perhaps span over many years to come. Softly, the rain began to fall.

It had now been a long time since the Great Race, and Indigo longed for more adventure and the new faces it would bring. The time had passed that Indigo could amuse himself for great lengths of time, and he often became bored and restless. The Wind, sensing the uneasiness of his little friend, thoughtfully tried to amuse Indigo with his stories. But sometimes, as you and I know, the Wind's job is rather dull, so boredom is something that even beautifully told stories couldn't counteract forever.

Indigo gazed at the majestic shoreline that the Wind had taken him to visit. The twosome had been drifting for days now, and he had seen the view many times. The sky felt different today, however—the deep blue possessing an eerie quality. The sea, too, was powerful and relentless. Watching its endless waves curl and crash made Indigo feel cold and anxious The Wind and the Sea knew one another well, as they had become dependent on each other through years of acquaintance. Today, the old friends chatted at great length about the old days when times were easier and they were younger. The sea complained about having trash thrown into him, and the Wind acknowledged that he had to work harder in recent times to blow away the smoke that filled the air over the cities.
The conversation grew boring for the little balloon as he glanced around for some other kind of amusement.

Above the old friends the sky had begun to darken and grow heavy. The Sea pondered carefully aloud, "It is to our disadvantage, my friend, that the moon is so unpredictable…" The wind agreed with his silence.

"What do you mean?" interrupted Indigo rudely. The kindly sea, polite as he was, launched into an explanation that, to this day, remains confusing to Indigo.

"The Moon and the Earth pull at me in such a way to cause my waves to curl and crash. It is difficult for me, and your friend here, to know when the Moon will be up to his nasty tricks again."

"Nasty tricks?" he questioned. "What tricks?"

Very quietly, the Wind answered, "Tidal waves and hurricanes."

"But what's a hurricane?" asked Indigo bluntly.

"SHHHHHH!!" both the Wind and the Sea exploded.

"Do you want to upset things?" demanded the Wind crossly. Indigo blushed and felt truly uneasy about his behavior, but still very curious. What could be so fearful about a hurricane that it would cause his teacher to become so edgy?

"Well," said the Wind, glancing worriedly up at the sky, "I think it is time that Indigo and I move on. Thank you, Sea, for the bit of conversation. Goodbye!"

"Yes, I believe that is best," said the Sea with concern in his voice, "Goodbye to you both, as well."

Indigo and the Wind prepared to move on, but in an instant Indigo was whisked over the jagged cliffs and out of sight of the Sea. The Wind was nearly dragging him along. It pained Indigo to go this fast, and his blue shell was beginning to flush with exhaustion.

"Please stop, Wind!" He protested, "I need to catch my breath!"

"Come along, Indigo!" snapped the Wind, "You mustn't dawdle." But a strange thing was beginning to happen to the balloon even as the Wind spoke. The faster he tried to catch up with the Wind the harder it was to move. He was being pushed by some strange force in the other direction, back towards the Sea and jagged cliffs. The trees began to bend and bow, the sand threw itself at the balloon, stinging his fragile shell.

"Wind!" cried Indigo anxiously, "I can't move! Wind! Where are you? WIIIIND!" But the Wind could not hear him, for it, too, seemed frantically caught up in the strange force, struggling to get free. Indigo felt himself being flipped about like a pancake. Below him, the kindly Sea, with whom he had spoken just minutes before, was a churning mass of explosions and waves. It had begun innocently enough, but now millions of pounds of water crashed against the cliffs and sands. It was a horrible sight, powerful Wind and mighty Sea clashing fiercely. Within moments, the noise was deafening, the sight chaotic, and Indigo was caught in the middle of the two.

"Help me!" Screamed Indigo at the air. But the rush of the Wind and the waves around him drowned out his words. He felt sick to his stomach from the tossing and turning. His blue sphere began to turn greenish, and he was afraid he might die. Where was the Wind? Why would he do this to him? Why had the two old friends suddenly become such enemies? The little balloon clutched his sphere with his tattered string feeling lonely, panicked, and wildly out of control.

Every breath was a struggle, and the moments dragged by like hours. If only Indigo could make it to a tree and wrap himself around it, at least until this stops. He tried futilely for a few minutes to steer his shape toward a tree that was now bending so low it touched the ground. It was no use—the raging force had a gripping control of the Wind, the Sea, and of course, Indigo.

Briefly, the tiny balloon was knocked into the tormented waters. His shape bobbled helplessly, the frigid waters were relentless. As he gasped for breath, he felt cold and sick. The waves crashed and churned over his head, as he struggled excruciatingly for air.

It could have been hours, perhaps days that passed with the Wind and the Sea at odds with each other. It was hard to tell. Indigo only struggled to stay alive. He would momentarily lose consciousness, only to awaken, confused and aching.

It was just when the exhausted balloon felt that he could hold on no longer that the force began to subside slightly. There was somewhat of a pause, a hesitation of the Wind, and what sounded like a *swishh, swishh, swishh* kind of sigh from the Sea. In that moment, Indigo weakly made his way to a nearby tree, crippled and exhausted from the event. He clung to the small tree, hugging its twisted and tattered trunk with his lifeless string.

It was a struggle to keep a hold of the tree, but gradually the force began to melt away. The Wind stilled. The Sea's waves began to topple gently over one another. The trees peered from beneath their branches and slowly stood up. And then, all went silent.

In the still of the moment, Indigo dozed off. His dreams were tangled and vivid, and he slept fitfully through the night. Time and sleep were on his side. The rays of the sun were barely peeking through the clouds when Indigo awoke. A faint groan sadly filled the air around him, and then went, once again, strangely still and silent. Something felt desperately wrong. Stumbling through the air he called, "Wind, where are you? Please answer me! Where are you?" How could the Wind do this to me, he thought. Panicked and frightened, he called again, but there was no answer. He searched as far as his ragged body would take him, sobbing uncontrollably. Fear gripped his heart and chilled him with anger and bitterness.

It was a long time before the groaning sound returned again, filling the air. It spoke weakly to Indigo. "I am weak, Indigo…. I must…. rest. . ."

There was nothing the little balloon could do except wait. And wait he did. The hours ticked away like days. He thought of all the Wind had taught him and the lovely stories he had told to pass the time. He reflected on the Wind's kindness, and his unfailing patience. He thought of all the times that he had been a nuisance to his great teacher, and vowed that if he ever had the chance, he would make it up to the Wind. He felt lonely and heartbroken. Silence echoed all around him.

It was near the end of the second day when he felt a rustle of his string and a faint tap on his shoulder. A familiar and loving tap. Yes, it was the Wind. Faithful, wise, ever-present Wind.

I believe there has never been a balloon so happy as Indigo was at that moment. Never was a sound more welcoming than the faint rustle of his string and the whisper of the Wind all around. It was indeed a time of thankfulness and rejoicing. He tossed his bright blue shape into the air with a song and a dance. The Wind chuckled weakly, the Sea lapped quietly at his makeshift string, and Indigo beamed into the brilliant sunshine.

"What is that melody?" asked the Wind groggily, not long after his ordeal. "Indigo, look below and tell me where we are." Indigo obediently looked below him and saw a sight that filled him with warmth and happiness. He saw warm, whitened beaches and a quiet, green ocean, lazily rolling its water onto a shore of expectant seagulls. The breeze was soft and warm, long stemmed trees with grass hats rocked gently in the Wind's kind air. Children in bright clothing sang and danced on the sandy beached, playing games with the sleepy ocean. Kites flew from the picketed fences that stood near by and teetered in the breeze. Indigo sighed as he began to tell the Wind of all that he saw below.

"Ahhh, yes," said the Wind with a bit more strength, "we are almost there." The Wind settled back to rest some more and said nothing to explain himself. Indigo tried not to be rude or disrespectful of the Wind, but more often than not his curiosity got the better of him.

"Where are we, Wind?"

The Wind, bothered, but not unaccustomed to the curious balloon's questions, answered, "So, you hear that lovely music?" Indigo nodded. "That comes from the marriage ceremony of two young people who are friends of the Wind and the Sky. We have been invited as honored guests for this occasion. I must admit, however, that after our ordeal, the event had temporarily slipped my mind. Come along now, Indigo, we mustn't be late." With that, the Wind mustered up all of his strength and gently pushed Indigo in the direction of the lightly twinkling melody.

"A marriage." Indigo thought, "What a lovely way to spend such a beautiful afternoon!"

"The young people I speak of," continued the Wind as they hurried along the streets of the village, "fly airplanes which require only my wind power to move. In the course of time, this young couple and I have seen a great deal together, both successes and failures." It was not hard for Indigo to tell that he felt very proud and honored indeed to be invited to this marriage.

Through the village the Wind and the little balloon flew; the music seemed to beckon them to their destination. Down the market place they flew, where vendors sold fresh fruits and vegetables, down past the park and over to a garden filled with flowers and smells that filled the air. Below, Indigo saw throngs of people all dressed in white garments with colorful sashes about their waists. Music exuded from these singers, strumming instruments and shaking gourds, creating a delightful rhythmic piece. The Wind, in his usual unassuming way, announced his arrival by gently rustling the long white dresses of the women. One man stood apart and shouted joyfully to the Wind and Indigo. He waved for the others to begin the ceremony.

There was absolute silence in the garden as the members of the wedding party took their places. Three singers began to sing softly. The moment sent a shiver of excitement through Indigo's sphere. A most beautiful woman with blue-black hair held back with tiny wispy flowers entered, gracefully walking down the garden path. Words from a language Indigo could not understand were spoken, two golden rings were presented. In some ways it appeared to be a rather sad occasion, but he couldn't help but think that whoever had invented weddings had created something even better than a round of Biddle Dee Bops on a starlit evening. Indigo had to keep silent for what seemed like a very long time. It wasn't until the newly married couple walked back up the path that there was a burst of excitement from the crowd and the festivities began!

Suddenly, the music sounded joyously, corks began popping everywhere and the people sang and danced gleefully among the flowers and music. Indigo rocked among them on the Wind's soft breeze as he, too, was caught up in the joyousness of the occasion.

Near the musicians, there stood a table laden with food of all kinds. Fresh flowers adorned the table and near the side, floating in the breeze, waved a child's abandoned balloon. It was a brilliant, rose-colored balloon that made Indigo blink in disbelief. The rosy balloon was searching for someone when she, too, caught sight of Indigo. They stared briefly and then turned away in embarrassment. The Wind nudged Indigo closer to the dainty balloon until he was floating next to her. His mouth fell open clear to his knot as he unabashedly stared at her. He thought she had the most wonderful shape and color he had ever seen on a balloon. Even Lawanda, in her striking lime-green color, could not match this balloon. Her knot, so firmly tied, gave her a sense of strength that complimented her airy glow. She seemed warm and gentle, with eyes that twinkled and a defiant mouth. She was someone, Indigo thought, who would make a very fine friend.

It was at this point that Indigo became very conscious of his own appearance. Slowly he glanced down at his own shell, not wishing to see what he knew was true—his lopsided shape, his weak knot, his tattered shirt tail for a string, the strange blue color that he knew swept all the way from his knot to the funny little lump at the top of his head. Tears flooded his eyes and a lump formed in his throat.

I must get out of here, he thought. I mustn't let her see me like this! I cannot let anyone so beautiful see me, one so tattered and old! I am nothing but a poor, shabby balloon with little more than an old man's shirttail to hold me together. He shot his angry words at the Wind, "How could you do that? How could you let her see me, Wind?"

He wanted to escape, to hide, and to be anywhere but under the examining eyes he had just met. Instantly, the tiny balloon turned and fled from the scene. Back through the garden he went, over the flowers and the music and the people, through the streets of the village, past the vendors who sold fresh fruits and vegetables, up the hill and over to the quiet, sandy beaches and lazy, green ocean. He watched the waves topple one on top of the other. He remembered the day of the hurricane and the angry tormented waters. This time Indigo felt that the waves were pounding *inside* him. The air inside of him seemed to ache and scream to be let out. All around him the Wind sighed.

After a long while, the Wind spoke. "Indigo, there is no need to feel ashamed, for you have grown in beauty. The air inside of you was lovingly given to you because you have learned devotion and compassion for your friends. Your color is as dark and strong as the mighty Sea itself. Your shape has given you the courage to live and learn as no other balloon

48

has. And your tattered shirttail is a message to the entire world that you have fought many battles and have won against the odds. You have found love, courage and identity."

"An identity." thought Indigo. "I have an Identity?"

He replied slowly and deliberately, trying hard not to let his voice quiver as obviously as his whole self, "Why then do I feel afraid for her to look at me, Wind? If what you say is so, why do I fear that she will not understand what you do, and she will laugh at me?" Anxiously, Indigo waited for a wise reply.

"If she behaves that way, then she is not as beautiful as she appears to be."

Indigo looked up, wiping away tears that stained his deep blue color. At a distance, behind a tree, shone the brilliant pink shape—the rosy color, the firm knot, the defiant mouth, that when added together would make a fine friend indeed (if only they might be given the chance).

He ventured near the balloon with all the courage and dignity that a little balloon could muster.

"My name is Indigo," he said boldly, extending his string to shake hers. "I …he stammered, "I would like very much for you to be my friend." Shyly, she looked up and smiled,

"My name is Scarlet, and yes, that would be lovely. I would like to be your friend."

"Really?" He gawked? "You don't mind being my friend? Are you certain?"

"Well, of course I am certain," said Scarlet, a little puzzled by the question. "I have been bored and lonely since going to live with my master, a little boy. He doesn't like to do much. And he hates to hum." She said the last statement quietly, her eyes darting around as if someone would hear her admission.

"Hum?" said Indigo, "You couldn't mean Biddle Dee Bops, could you?"

"Why yes! I do mean Biddle Dee Bops! However did you know?"

A smile spread across Indigo's face that reached from one side to the other; a friend who like to hum, a fine friend indeed. A surge of happiness began to fill him up, until he thought he might explode. It filled his heart, his soul, his being. The Wind chuckled a deep, loving chuckle as he watched Scarlet and Indigo sing a joyful chorus of Biddle Dee Bops. It was the beginning of something new—a bountiful celebration, light winds to carry them, a lovely new friend.

Even the Sea seemed to be singing quietly along with the tune:

And then we three

(Biddle dee bop)

Can sail the seas

(Biddle dee bop)

And go as we please

You two and me.

51

About the Creators

Kathryn Phillips is an internationally recognized speaker and consultant with over thirty years of experience in education. Among her unique qualifications, she is a mother, experienced educator, behavior specialist, school administrator, published author and college professor. She has taken particular delight in sharing the Adventures of Indigo with elementary children around the world, since the story first began more than 35 years ago when she lived and schooled in London. Kathryn is the President and Founder of Total Behavior Management and Phillips Associates, LLC. She is available for onsite consultation, keynotes speeches, workshops and presentations on a variety of behavior management and educational issues. For further information log onto www.totalbehaviormanagement.com, or call 800-810-3610.

Julia Reynolds was born in San Francisco. She has lived in San Diego, Hawaii, and Germany, and currently calls Bend, Oregon her home. Julia received a BA in Studio Art from the University of Oregon in 2005. *The Adventures of Indigo* is her first published children's book. Being creative and making art has always been an important part of her life. She credits the love and support of her mother, Catherine, a teacher and artist, for helping her to become the person she is today. Like Indigo, Julia hopes to have many more adventures.

Steven Talbott is an elementary school teacher who taught for years in a one-room schoolhouse in rural Oregon. Through working with students K-8 in that setting, he has developed a unique ability to differentiate instruction to meet the needs of a wide range of learners. He has a passion for bringing out Language Arts skills and abilities in students and can attest to the benefit of providing developmentally appropriate methods and materials in order to maximize student achievement in all subjects. He currently resides in beautiful Bend, Oregon with his wife and two children.